The Stewardship Series 1

CARETAKERS OF GOD'S BLESSINGS

Using Our Resources Wisely

The Stewardship Series 1

CARETAKERS OF GOD'S BLESSINGS

Using Our Resources Wisely

LARRY BURKETT

Edited and Arranged by Karen C. Lee-Thorp

Edited by Adeline Griffith, Christian Financial Concepts

ISBN: 0-8024-2805-3

3 5 7 9 10 8 6 4 2

Printed in the United States of America

TABLE OF CONTENTS

USING THIS STUDY GUIDE

Learning to handle money and possessions is one of the most important things we can do for our spiritual growth. Our use of money both reflects and greatly affects the true state of our relationship with God. But money is a touchy subject—rarely discussed in pulpits or even in small groups—so many people are simply unaware of how much insight the Bible offers into handling money wisely.

The Stewardship Series of study guides is designed to help you learn and practice the basic biblical principles of handling wealth, whether you have a lot or a very little. A *steward* is someone who manages another person's property; God has entrusted every one of us with resources to manage for His purposes. When we understand God's goals and methods, managing money can become an exciting adventure instead of a confusing burden.

Caretakers of God's Blessings addresses God's financial priorities and investment philosophy—His views on managing a household, as well as the entire earth. You'll learn the kinds of questions to ask yourself when making a financial decision and the enormous difference it makes when you acknowledge God's ownership of all your possessions.

First of all, this guide is designed with small groups in mind. Money is an intensely private matter, and you won't be asked to divulge information inappropriately, but teaming up with a group of like-minded people offers you the chance to learn from others and receive their encouragement. However, you can easily adapt *Caretakers of God's Blessings* for use with just one other person or even use it on your own. If you are helping someone else learn to manage his or her finances, you may find the guides in this series to be a helpful part of what you do together. Engaged and married couples also will find these guides invaluable in sorting out how to handle their finances jointly.

The following elements are included in the sessions.

Approach Question(s). Most sessions begin with one or two questions that invite participants to share what they've been thinking and feeling about money during the week. These questions often refer to the homework assignment from the previous session. Group members have a chance to share with each other what they have learned from the homework exercise.

Teaching and Scripture. Next there are several pages of teaching on a topic, built around a few key passages of Scripture. Ideally, participants should have read and digested this section before coming to the group meeting; but, the text is brief enough to take ten minutes to read it during the meeting. Key paragraphs and Scripture passages could be reread during the meeting in order to discuss the questions.

Discussion Questions. These questions invite you to respond to the teaching and Scripture. Two people probably could cover them in twenty minutes; eight or ten people could use an hour, although forty minutes would be adequate. Some questions may provoke such a lively discussion that the leader will have to decide whether to cut off the discussion and move on or skip some of the later questions. When a question is personal, you always have the option of writing a full answer on your own and telling the group only what you feel is appropriate.

The Grace Adventure. Each session closes with a reminder that God's grace is available to accomplish what God's Word asks of us. God doesn't issue a lot of commands and leave us to fend for ourselves.

This section also includes a suggestion for how to pray in response to what you've been discussing. Prayer is a way of acknowledging and seeking God's grace. If your group is accustomed to praying together, you may not need the suggestions to guide your prayers.

If some participants are unaccustomed to praying aloud, you may decide to make your prayer time brief, allow time for silent prayer only, or let some pray aloud and others remain silent. Decide on the ground rules for group prayer at your first meeting so no one will fear being put on the spot later on.

During the Week. A Bible study guide typically asks you to study one or more Bible passages in preparation for your next group meeting. By contrast, this guide asks you to reflect on one or two of the verses you have just discussed. The idea is to let those key truths sink into your mind and heart.

You'll also be asked to pay attention to the way you handle money during the week, in light of what you have been discussing. Meditating on Scripture and observing your own behavior work together to help you really listen to what God is telling you to do.

Prayer will be a part of this listening. Finally, you'll be asked to read the teaching for the next session. If you only have time either to read the next session or do the other homework activities, choose the meditating and observing. However, reading ahead should take you only about ten minutes and will save a lot of time during your group meeting.

I trust that the Holy Spirit will guide you to examine your financial life through the teaching of God's Word.

* * * *

"Blessed is the man who fears the Lord, who finds great delight in his commands. His children will be mighty in the land; the generation of the upright will be blessed. Wealth and riches are in his house, and his righteousness endures forever" (Psalm 112:1–3)

"Two things I ask of you, O Lord; do not refuse me before I die: Keep falsehood and lies far from me; give me neither poverty nor riches, but give me only my daily bread. Otherwise, I may have too much and disown you and say, 'Who is the Lord?' Or I may become poor and steal, and so dishonor the name of my God" (Proverbs 30:7–9)

GOD'S COLLEAGUES

Management

For most of us, the word *stewardship* suggests images of church fund-raising, if it suggests any images at all. We don't use the word much these days in ordinary conversation. *Management*, however, we are all familiar with. A manager in a business oversees the use of some portion of the company's resources—money, machinery, personnel—in order to produce a product or service in line with the company's values.

If a shoe manufacturer, for instance, values high quality and low cost, the factory manager thinks about how to obtain the best leather at the least cost and how to train the employees most cost effectively. If the shoe company also values employee satisfaction, the manager also thinks about the work environment, schedules, child care, and benefits.

On a larger scale, the Bureau of Land Management (BLM), in the U.S. Department of the Interior, manages land owned by the U.S. government. The BLM regulates timber harvesting, livestock grazing, and recreation according to values and priorities set by Congress and the president, with input from citizens. BLM employees don't own the land and aren't supposed to manage it for their own gain; they are supposed to manage it according to the best interests of all U.S. citizens—both those living now and those yet to be born.

According to the Bible, God created the planet Earth and consequently owns it lock, stock, and barrel: *"The earth is the Lord's, and everything in it, the world, and all who live in it; for he founded it upon the seas and established it upon the waters"* (Psalm 24:1–2).

God created humans to manage this magnificent estate: *"So God created man in his own image, in the image of God he created him; male and female he created them. God blessed them and said to them, 'Be fruitful and increase in number; fill the earth and subdue it. Rule over the fish of the sea and the birds of the air and over every living creature that moves on the ground.' The Lord God took the man and put him in the Garden of Eden to work it and take care of it"* (Genesis 1:27–28; 2:15).

What does it mean to be created in God's image? The answer is huge, but at least in part it means we have the potential to be full partners with God in cultivating His vast garden. We are not mindless slaves executing menial tasks; we are gifted managers equipped to oversee resources creatively in order to produce what God values.

In the day-to-day tussles of life, it's easy to lose sight of our huge and honorable responsibility as managers or stewards of God's property. Since God has divided the job among so many of us, most of us have direct responsibility for what seems like only a tiny amount of resources.

Consider Neil and Diane. If you were to ask Neil what resources God has asked him to manage, at first he would look at you blankly. He's aware of owning a car, having about $18,000 of equity in a home (as well as a much larger mortgage), owning some furniture and electronics, and having a few thousand dollars in the bank, but he doesn't think of those as resources he's managing on God's behalf.

Neil thinks those are *his* possessions. With a little help he could calculate *his* net worth, and it would look pretty paltry. It's no wonder Neil gravitates to the car magazines. Wouldn't he feel successful if he drove one of those machines! And it's no wonder he knocks himself out at work, trying to get ahead. Neil needs to prove he's somebody, that he's achieving something significant, even if it's only having the highest sales quota in his division. Neil has no idea he has an enormously responsible position in the business of the universe.

How would Neil's life change if he understood how things really stand? What appear to be his possessions, for his enjoyment alone, are really God's possessions, to be managed according to God's values and in pursuit of God's extremely important agenda. Far from stripping Neil of what matters most to him, this perspective actually gives him a dignity he never knew he possessed. God's agenda is not merely to keep Neil's family reasonably comfortable. God has a kingdom to build.

The Kingdom of God

God gave Adam and Eve the job of managing His estate, but they disobeyed His instructions. Since then, human beings have been mismanaging God's planet with disastrous results. We act as if we own whatever we can hold onto and that we get to set the values by which we use it.

God says weak people are as valuable as strong people,

and all people are more valuable than a few people's financial gain, but we have ignored those values and set our own. We've had terrible management advice from Satan. The Bible calls this state of affairs *"the dominion of darkness"* (Colossians 1:13).

When Jesus came to earth, He announced that the kingdom of God had arrived because He, the King, had arrived. The term *kingdom of God,* or its equivalent, *kingdom of heaven,* appears dozens of times in the Gospels. It refers to the time of God's dominion or reign on earth, when everything works according to God's values. The Jews expected a regal, majestic King to ride in and take over by force, subjecting everyone to His rule. Instead, Jesus came humbly and asked people to submit to His rule voluntarily.

We are supposed to acknowledge Jesus as the rightful owner of the resources we manage. The time will come when this chance to acknowledge Jesus voluntarily is past, but until then we all get to make daily choices. As the King's voluntary subjects, our job is to manage our resources according to God's values and to accomplish His will according to His Word.

In that respect, Neil and Diane have an opportunity to use their resources to achieve God's agenda: to build His kingdom. The resources God has entrusted to them include not just their material possessions but also their innate abilities, knowledge, learned skills, and relationships. Everything, from the dirt in their backyard to their minds and bodies, is a resource to be managed for God. They don't have to waste time trying to prove they're important; they already *are* important: members of God's management team.

Building the kingdom would sound like a nice idea to Neil and Diane if they had the time and money for it. Unfortunately, Neil has a sales quota to meet, Diane has clients all day, one of their kids needs glasses, another needs braces, and the mortgage is just a bit higher than they really can afford. If God owns everything, couldn't He give Diane a raise and do something about the medical bills?

Diane and Neil need to understand that building the kingdom isn't just "ministry" as it's commonly understood—something missionaries, pastors, Sunday school teachers, youth workers, and evangelists do out there in the public arena. It includes preaching, teaching, and healing, but it begins with work inside us.

"Once, having been asked by the Pharisees when the kingdom of God would come, Jesus replied, 'The kingdom of God does not come with your careful observation, nor will people say, "Here it is," or "There it is," because the kingdom of God is within you'" (Luke 17:20–21).

"The acts of the sinful nature are obvious: sexual immorality, impurity and debauchery; idolatry and witchcraft; hatred, discord, jealousy, fits of rage, selfish ambition, dissensions, factions and envy; drunkenness, orgies, and the like. I warn you, as I did before, that those who live like this will not inherit the kingdom of God. But the fruit of the Spirit is love, joy, peace, patience, kindness, goodness, faithfulness, gentleness and self-control. Against such things there is no law" (Galatians 5:19–23).

Thus, a big part of Neil and Diane's kingdom building will involve cooperating with God's Spirit as He tears down anger and selfish ambition inside each of them and builds up love, peace, and the other traits of the inner kingdom. Wise management of their financial resources will include investing in pursuits that foster inner growth.

At the same time, the more the Holy Spirit builds the kingdom within them, the more wisdom, peace, and love they will have to guide them in decisions about household expenses, career choices, and so on. Decisions like these will build God's kingdom in Diane and Neil's family and also will equip them to build the kingdom beyond their front door.

I've found that a key to my sense of peace and my ability to make clear and wise choices is consciously to hand over ownership of my resources to God. This decision is a cornerstone of inner kingdom building. Neil and Diane don't have enough time and money *not* to take this step. The alternative to inner and outer kingdom building is our modern rat race that leads nowhere.

What Do You Think?

1. What do you think of the above definition of
   stewardship? Does it surprise you? Appeal to you?
   Why?

_____

_____

_____

2. What experience do you have with managing
   resources in your personal life, a family, or a
   business?

_____

_____

_____

_____

3. Can you identify with Neil or Diane in any ways? How are you like or unlike them?

_____

_____

_____

_____

4. What do you think God means when He says to "subdue" the earth, "rule" over the animals, and "take care of" the land? What does that mean in practical terms?

_____

_____

_____

_____

5. What would you like to know from God about your job as manager of part of His property? List all the questions you would like to ask God about this.

_____

_____

_____

_____

_____

_____

6. a. Many businesses have an annual meeting in which managers report to stockholders how well they have managed the company's assets. In our case, God is the only stockholder. Imagine you were to meet tomorrow with God to report on how you are doing as a manager. How do you envision Him responding to your report? Check one of the following.

❏ He'd be furious. He'd chew me out and then fire me.

❏ He'd be quietly disappointed and leave, sadly shaking His head.

❏ He'd ask probing questions, spend an hour coaching me on areas where I need help, and make an appointment to meet again in a week to see how I'm doing.

❏ He'd pat me on the back for doing such a great job and give me a raise.

❏ Other (Describe what you'd expect.)

_____

_____

_____

b. Why would you expect God to respond in that way?

_____

_____

_____

7. What is one way in which being God's managers might affect the way Neil and Diane make decisions about their resources? (We'll consider this question in more detail in future sessions.)

_____

_____

_____

8. What do you hope to get out of this study on managing God's resources?

_____

_____

_____

If Neil and Diane are managing God's money, their first task is to find out what God values, what God wants done, and how their resources can best serve that agenda. Then, with that agenda in mind, their job is to start managing. They'll probably want to consult the Bible, which lays out God's agenda in detail. They'll also team up with others who are managing God's resources.

The rest of the sessions in this guide are designed to help people like Neil and Diane team up and learn together some basic biblical principles of resource management. That's what *stewardship* is about.

The Grace Adventure

When we first begin to grasp our job description, it can feel overwhelming. A planet to manage! A kingdom to build! On the other hand, it can feel exciting. The difference is grace. In the Bible, *grace* refers to two generous gifts God gives us. One is the welcoming forgiveness He offers us when we fall far short of His standard for a wise and loving life, when we fail to manage His resources well. The other is the empowering presence of the Holy Spirit within us, the Spirit who can enable us to become far more effective managers and kingdom-builders than we ever dreamed of being.

Unless we believe firmly that God extends unlimited grace to us, we likely will feel more overwhelmed than excited by the task we face. But if we believe in grace, our responsibility as stewards can become the first step in an adventure of living by grace.

9. If your group is larger than five, divide into groups

of three. Tell your partners how you're feeling about
this business of being God's manager. Also, tell one
thing you'd like them to pray for. Maybe you have a
question about what all this means for your life.
Maybe you're facing a particular financial decision.
Maybe you'd like to pray for forgiving grace or
empowering grace.

When each of you has shared, allow a few minutes
for prayer. If you're unaccustomed to praying aloud
with others, it's okay to pray silently or to pray just
one sentence. If you prefer, one member of your
subgroup could volunteer to pray for all three of you.

During the Week

- Copy onto a card or sheet of notepaper: *"The Lord
  God took the man and put him in the Garden of Eden
  to work it and take care of it"* (Genesis 2:15).

  Post it where you will see it often during the
  week—perhaps on your dashboard, refrigerator, or
  desk. When you see it, think about your job as a
  manager of God's resources to build His kingdom.
  Think of what this might mean for you.

- Something amazing happens inside us when we
  accept our role as managers of God's assets and
  transfer ownership of everything we possess to
  God. Take a few minutes this week to be alone
  with God. Tell Him you are transferring
  ownership of all your resources to Him. List the
  major items, if you find that helpful. Consider
  writing down your commitment and dating it.

- Finally, read "Priorities" in session 2 (pages 23–24). Does it make sense? Do you disagree with anything there? What questions does it raise for you? Your group will make more progress if everyone has taken time to read this section.

WHAT GOD VALUES

1. Explain how it felt to tell God He could take charge of everything you own. Was it a relief? Scary?

_____

_____

_____

If you didn't get a chance to pray about transferring ownership to God, think about it now. How does it feel when you think about doing that?

_____

_____

_____

Priorities

So we've established that everything we have really belongs to God. What does that mean in day-to-day, practical terms? In order to manage God's resources well, we have to know what His goals are.

Suppose Neil and Diane are thinking of buying a car and want to know what car I would recommend. In order to advise them, I would have to know their goals. Fuel efficiency? Space for two adults and four children?

Safety? High performance? A sporty appearance? Leather upholstery? Total cost below $12,000? Chances are that they won't find one car that meets all of these criteria, so they will have to rank them in order of priority. If they have four children, they may have to rank dependability and interior space above the appearance.

In the same way, we need to know what God wants us to spend His money on. Thus, in any given situation it's essential to pray: Is this a good decision? Should I buy a new car or keep my current one for another couple of years? We need to develop the habit of praying consistently about financial decisions. If we're serious about treating our resources as belonging ultimately to God, we won't settle for a quick "Show me the right car, Lord" and go about our business. Instead, we'll develop a lifestyle of prayer.

However, even diligent prayer about specific decisions is no substitute for a basic working knowledge of God's financial priorities. If we already know the kinds of things God values a great deal and the kinds of things He considers relatively unimportant, many financial decisions will be fairly obvious. There's no point in praying, "God, should I buy this gram of cocaine?" and then sitting around waiting for a voice from heaven. God has already laid out His priorities in the Bible, so it is the first place we should go when we want guidance from Him.

We cannot hope to cover all of God's financial priorities in one study session, but we can learn to ask the right kinds of questions when we investigate the Scriptures. Consider Jesus' parable about how the King of God's kingdom will assess His subjects.

"When the Son of Man comes in his glory, and all the angels with him, he will sit on his throne in heavenly glory. All the nations will be gathered before him, and he will separate the people one from another as a shepherd separates the sheep from the goats. He will put the sheep on his right and the goats on his left.

"Then the King will say to those on his right, 'Come, you who are blessed by my Father; take your inheritance, the kingdom prepared for you since the creation of the world. For I was hungry and you gave me something to eat, I was thirsty and you gave me something to drink, I was a stranger and you invited me in, I needed clothes and you clothed me, I was sick and you looked after me, I was in prison and you came to visit me.'

"Then the righteous will answer him, 'Lord, when did we see you hungry and feed you, or thirsty and give you something to drink? When did we see you a stranger and invite you in, or needing clothes and clothe you? When did we see you sick or in prison and go to visit you?'

"The King will reply, 'I tell you the truth, whatever you did for one of the least of these brothers of mine, you did for me.'

"Then he will say to those on his left, 'Depart from me, you who are cursed, into the eternal fire prepared for the devil and his angels. For I was hungry and you gave me nothing to eat, I was thirsty and you gave me nothing to drink, I was a stranger and you did not invite me in, I needed clothes and you did not clothe me, I was sick and in prison and you did not look after me.'

"They also will answer, 'Lord, when did we see you hungry or thirsty or a stranger or needing clothes or sick or in prison, and did not help you?' He will reply, 'I tell you the truth, whatever you did not do for one of the least of these, you did not do for me.' Then they will go away to eternal punishment, but the righteous to eternal life" (Matthew 25:31–46).

2. What does this parable tell you about the King's financial priorities? What does He think it is important for His subjects to spend their resources on—both money and abilities?

_____

_____

_____

_____

Now consider some of the apostle Paul's instructions: "Give proper recognition to those widows who are really in need. But if a widow has children or grandchildren, these should learn first of all to put their religion into practice by caring for their own family and so repaying their parents and grandparents, for this is pleasing to God.

"The widow who is really in need and left all alone puts her hope in God and continues night and day to pray and to ask God for help. But the widow who lives for pleasure is dead even while she lives.

"Give the people these instructions, too, so that no one may be open to blame. If anyone does not provide for his relatives, and especially for his immediate family, he has denied the faith and is worse than an unbeliever" (1 Timothy 5:3–8).

3. What does this passage from 1 Timothy say about
   how God wants us to use His money?

_____

_____

_____

_____

Paul goes on to tell Timothy: "*But godliness with con-
tentment is great gain. For we brought nothing into the world,
and we can take nothing out of it. But if we have food and
clothing, we will be content with that. People who want to get
rich fall into temptation and a trap and into many foolish and
harmful desires that plunge men into ruin and destruction. For
the love of money is a root of all kinds of evil. Some people,
eager for money, have wandered from the faith and pierced
themselves with many griefs*" (1 Timothy 6:6–10).

4. What does this Scripture say are important and
   unimportant financial goals?

   Important:

_____

_____

_____

_____

Unimportant:

_____

_____

_____

_____

Jesus gave His followers a mission. A mission is the most important things we can possibly do with our time, money, and abilities. In the following two passages, Jesus defines His followers' mission.

"He called his twelve disciples to him and gave them authority to drive out evil spirits and to heal every disease and sickness. . . . These twelve Jesus sent out with the following instructions: . . . 'As you go, preach this message: "The kingdom of heaven is near." Heal the sick, raise the dead, cleanse those who have leprosy, drive out demons. Freely you have received, freely give'" (Matthew 10:1, 5–8).

"Then Jesus came to them and said, 'All authority in heaven and on earth has been given to me. Therefore go and make disciples of all nations, baptizing them in the name of the Father and of the Son and of the Holy Spirit, and teaching them to obey everything I have commanded you'" (Matthew 28:18–20).

5. According to those two passages, what are some of the things God really wants done in the world?

_____

_____

All of the above passages deal with what we might call *external* priorities—aspects of building God's kingdom out in the world. Just as important are God's *internal* priorities—ways He wants to build His kingdom inside us. Do you recall the following passage from session 1?

"The acts of the sinful nature are obvious: sexual immorality, impurity and debauchery; idolatry and witch- craft; hatred, discord, jealousy, fits of rage, selfish ambition, dissensions, factions and envy; drunkenness, orgies, and the like. I warn you, as I did before, that those who live like this will not inherit the kingdom of God. But the fruit of the Spirit is love, joy, peace, patience, kindness, goodness, faithful- ness, gentleness and self-control. Against such things there is no law" (Galatians 5:19–23).

6. What are some of God's internal priorities?

_____

_____

_____

7. This is just a quick sampling of Scripture. But from these few passages, what would you say God thinks are important financial priorities? What are some financial goals that He might view as okay but relatively unimportant?

Important financial priorities:

_____

_____

_____

_____

_____

Relatively unimportant goals:

_____

_____

_____

_____

_____

_____

It is sometimes tricky to apply what we read in the Scriptures to our modern situations. For example, Paul tells Timothy that the members of his church should be content with food and clothing. What about education for one's children? In the first century, only the very rich could afford any education other than training for a job like leather working or stonecutting.

In our much more complicated world, however, some would argue that computer literacy for young people is as essential for survival above the poverty line as food and clothing are. Others would argue that computer literacy is a luxury. Should Diane and Neil invest in a computer and drive older cars if they cannot afford both a computer and newer cars?

And what about giving to the poor? Diane might conclude that God wants her to supply food and clothing to a homeless shelter. Neil might decide the best thing he can do for the poor is to team up with some friends from church to buy used computers for a Christian school in the inner city and to volunteer one evening a week to train kids how to use them. If they were single, they might both be right about what God wants them to do with their money and time. But since they are married, they may have to discuss these decisions and come to some agreements.

Issues like these show why it is essential to search the Bible broadly for God's values, rather than basing all of our decisions on a few passages. But the most important thing is to develop the habit of asking the right questions: What does God value highly? What does He consider less important? How can I use my resources to produce the things God values highly? How much am I spending on things that are unimportant to God?

8. Take five minutes on your own to write down some of the questions you have about your own financial priorities. (You need not share this list with the group, so you can be completely candid.)

_____

_____

_____

_____

_____

_____

Maybe you've been considering buying a new car. Your list might include questions like these:

- How important is it to God that I drive a new car?
- Is a new car more important than something else I might do with that money?
- How will buying a new car affect my ability to feed and clothe my family?
- How will buying a new car affect my ability to heal the sick, spread the Gospel, or care for the needy?

9. Share with your group what you learned from making this list of questions. (You may or may not choose to share the questions themselves.)

The Grace Adventure

Probably no one in your group can afford to care adequately for an entire extended family, as well as meet all the needs of the poor and get the Gospel to the entire world. There is probably no limit to the amount of money and time you could spend on books, retreats, counseling, and spiritual disciplines in the pursuit of inner growth.

Nobody can do everything God wants done. Furthermore, it may take time to shift your priorities so they will reflect more of God's priorities. God is eager to forgive our indifference to His agenda and eager to coach us in shifting our priorities. All He asks is that we set our faces in the right direction and start moving ahead.

10. Divide into groups of three. Use your lists from question 8 as a basis for prayer. Ask God the questions on your list. Ask Him to forgive your misdirected priorities and give you wisdom and strength to discern and act on His priorities. Pray silently or aloud, as you choose.

During the Week

- Select a sentence or two from one of the Scripture passages in this session. Choose something you believe God wants you to make a priority. Copy your selected sentence(s) onto a card or sheet of notepaper, and post it along with Genesis 2:15.

- Set aside some time this week to read and think about your list from question 8. Pray about your list. Do you have any sense of answers from God? Is the Scripture passage you selected relevant in any ways? Consider discussing some of the questions on your list in number 8 with your spouse or a friend.

- Read session 3 before your next meeting.

RISKY BUSINESS

1. What is one financial priority you think you should pay more attention to than you have?

_____

_____

_____

God's Investment Philosophy

Knowing God's heart is just as important as knowing God's priorities. What kind of a Person is He? When you work for a boss, it pays to understand how he or she operates. When you are managing someone's money, it's wise to know if your client is willing to take big risks for possibly big returns or if your client is more concerned with avoiding any potential loss.

Jesus painted story-pictures of what God is like and how His kingdom operates. One of them concerned a man who owned eight "talents." A talent was a measure of weight: 75 pounds of silver. Eight talents was more wealth than most of Jesus' hearers were likely to see in their lifetimes. Even one talent was well beyond anything the average person could imagine possessing at one time. At that time, to be handed a talent of silver and asked to take care of it would have felt something like being given a quarter of a million dollars today for safekeeping.

"*Again,* [the kingdom of God] *will be like a man going on a journey, who called his servants and entrusted his property to them. To one he gave five talents of money, to another two talents, and to another one talent, each according to his ability. Then he went on his journey. The man who had received the five talents went at once and put his money to work and gained five more. So also, the one with the two talents gained two more. But the man who had received the one talent went off, dug a hole in the ground and hid his master's money.*

"*After a long time the master of those servants returned and settled accounts with them. The man who had received the five talents brought the other five. 'Master,' he said, 'you entrusted me with five talents. See, I have gained five more.'*

"*His master replied, 'Well done, good and faithful servant! You have been faithful with a few things; I will put you in charge of many things. Come and share your master's happiness!'*

"*The man with the two talents also came. 'Master,' he said, 'you entrusted me with two talents; see, I have gained two more.'*

"*His master replied, 'Well done, good and faithful servant! You have been faithful with a few things; I will put you in charge of many things. Come and share your master's happiness!'*

"*Then the man who had received the one talent came. 'Master,' he said, 'I knew that you are a hard man, harvesting where you have not sown and gathering where you have not scattered seed. So I was afraid and went out and hid your talent in the ground. See, here is what belongs to you.'*

"*His master replied, 'You wicked, lazy servant! So you knew that I harvest where I have not sown and gather where I have not scattered seed? Well then, you should have put my* money on deposit with the bankers, so that when I returned I would have received it back with interest.

"'Take the talent from him and give it to the one who has the ten talents. For everyone who has will be given more, and he will have an abundance. Whoever does not have, even what he has will be taken from him. And throw that worthless servant outside, into the darkness, where there will be weeping and gnashing of teeth'" (Matthew 25:14–30).

2. a. Put yourself in the place of the man entrusted with five talents. Your boss has given you over a million dollars of his money to take care of. How do you feel?

_____

_____

   b. What will you do?

_____

_____

_____

_____

3. a. Why did the servant with one talent bury it instead of investing it?

_____

_____

_____

b. What did that servant fail to understand about his master?

_____

_____

_____

c. What point do you think Jesus was making in this story?

_____

_____

_____

4. It's also interesting to notice how the master rewarded the servants who invested wisely: *"You have been faithful with a few things; I will put you in charge of many things."* More work! What does this dynamic tell you about how things operate in the kingdom of God?

_____

_____

_____

5. These days we don't use the word *talent* for literal money but for another kind of wealth: an innate ability. What wealth or resources has God entrusted to you? Give some examples.

The story of the talents relates to question 6 of session 1: "Imagine you were to meet tomorrow with God to report on how you are doing as a manager. How do you envision Him responding to your report?" If you envision Him as angry or aloof, you might handle His resources like the servant who saw his master as "a hard man." It's very difficult to take creative risks with God's resources if deep down you worry that God will be displeased if you fail.

6. a. Do you think we're working for the kind of employer who celebrates taking risks or playing it safe? Why do you say that?

---

   b. Do you see God as "a hard man"? Why or why not?

_____

_____

_____

7. To some degree, a taste for risk-taking is a matter of temperament. Some people thrive on risk, to their detriment, speculating wildly with their money and that of others. They love the adrenaline rush. Other people hate risks. Some crave excitement; others want security. Where are you on the risk scale?

0   1   2   3   4   5   6   7   8   9   10

_____

I hate risk   I love risk

For those who love risk, often the challenge is to channel that instinct into God's priorities, rather than just into feeling the rush or getting rich quick. I know one missionary named Kent who says if he hadn't gotten into God's business he probably would have found his way into the Mafia. Kent thinks big. Building an ordinary business isn't big enough. Making a lot of money isn't big enough. Becoming a celebrity or wielding authority over a huge organization isn't big enough. Only the kingdom of God is big enough.

Kent thinks so big, he's willing to spend his life in obscurity planting seeds that will grow into healthy trees ten or twenty years later. He thrives on figuring out how to get the Gospel into places most people have given up on.

For those who love security, on the other hand, the challenge is to believe in the God who harvests where He hasn't sown and gathers where He hasn't scattered seed. Many of us need to grasp that God has actually entrusted a princely sum to us and expects us to invest it courageously.

Neil has a fairly high tolerance for risk. Diane is more apt to worry about what may happen if a gamble doesn't pay off. Neil is confident of his ability to discern when to buy an investment and when to sell it, and he's pretty sharp in the short run. Diane, however, has a better instinct for long-term investments. Her trouble is that whenever one of her retirement funds has a bad six months, she agonizes over whether she made a mistake in choosing it.

Neil's inner work will include tempering his arrogance and putting more of his trust in God (and Diane's careful research). Diane needs to worry less and trust that if she has done her homework and prayed faithfully, God can provide for her family despite her occasional mistakes.

Diane has a chance to leave her current full-time job and work at home on a project that she would love. It fits her skills perfectly, and it's a job both she and Neil agree is consistent with God's values. However, there's no guaranteed salary. Diane wants to believe God will take care of her family if she changes jobs, but if she takes the risk and doesn't succeed, she knows she'll be looking for someone to blame: either God for not providing properly, herself for not hearing God properly, or Neil for talking her into taking the risk. This decision about managing her resources in the outer world is giving Diane a prime lesson in managing her inner world.

8. a. How would you suggest that Diane approach this decision?

_____

_____

_____

_____

   b. What do you think Neil should do?

_____

_____

_____

_____

9. Think of something you believe God wants done in your world: in your heart, in your household, or within twenty miles or so of where you live or work. What would you be risking if you invested some of your money, time, or other resources in that pursuit?

_____

_____

_____

_____

_____

The Grace Adventure

It's easy to feel ashamed that we're not doing enough to build God's kingdom. It's easy to berate ourselves for fearing risks or for preferring the wrong kinds of risks. But God is patient and eager to forgive us. None of our mistakes are too big for Him. He knows exactly how much wealth He has entrusted to each of us, and He believes in what we can do with it, with His help. His Holy Spirit lives inside us, eager to guide us in investing our resources wisely and courageously.

10. Divide into groups of three. Tell your partners what you're feeling. Inadequate? That's probably how all three servants felt. Tell your partners what this session prompts you to want to ask from God. Pray for your partners.

During the Week

- Copy and post this portion of Jesus's story: *"Well done, good and faithful servant! You have been faithful with a few things; I will put you in charge of many things. Come and share your master's happiness!"* (Matthew 25:21).

- Take some time this week to think about how you can be faithful with the few things God has entrusted to you.

- Read session 4 before your next meeting.

43

MANAGING MUCH OR LITTLE

1. Tell the group about one decision you have made since your last meeting that involved managing some of God's resources. What priorities were you trying to serve?

_____

_____

Planning for the Future

Diane believes in planning for the future. She and Neil have been saving for years for their two children's college education, even though she knows whatever they save won't be nearly enough to cover all the costs of private colleges. They also are saving for retirement so they won't have to work after they're sixty-five. If Diane had her way, they would save much more than they do. She knows that one of them might get sick and be unable to work, or one of the kids might have an accident. Tornadoes have been known to demolish houses in their part of the country, and Neil and Diane have a beautiful home. They've put a lot of money and effort into that home, and Diane would be sick if anything happened to it.

Neil worries less than Diane about the future; he's more interested in living the good life now. He feels he works hard to be able to afford things he enjoys: things with sleek lines and state-of-the-art circuitry. To him, a car or computer older than three years is obsolete.

Neil and Diane don't feel rich; they feel they're just getting by. Raising children is expensive. A four-bedroom home and two fairly new cars require maintenance. When their church elders talk every year about "stewardship" (translate: fund-raising) and "tithing," Neil and Diane squirm. They believe that they'll never be able to afford to give 10 percent of their income to the church—not in a lifetime!

Sharon, a single mother of three who works with Diane, cringes internally when Diane talks about mutual funds and college savings. She's lucky if she can afford school clothes, and she feels guilty that she can't give her kids what the other kids in their classes have: Nintendo, music lessons, CD-ROM. After being in Diane's home for a Christmas party, Sharon would be too embarrassed to invite Diane to her place. Sharon doesn't think about retiring; she hopes to stay healthy enough to work until she drops dead so she won't be a burden to her kids. Retirement? Sharon would be happy to be able to afford vacations.

Two decades ago, most Americans could legitimately call themselves middle class. However, although a variety of economic shifts have helped some people like Neil and Diane prosper abundantly, many others, like Sharon, fall further and further behind. Sharon will never own a home, a car less than four years old, or a computer; nor will she have new furniture. She can't afford to live in a good school district, so the chances of her children doing well enough to win college financial aid are slim, and without college degrees their prospects in our economy are dim. Even with degrees, they will struggle.

Diane is like the servant entrusted with five talents; Sharon has only one talent to work with. Both women need to learn to manage the resources entrusted to them, but the challenges they face are not entirely the same. Jesus lived in a society in which the gap between rich and poor was even wider than it is in ours, so when He taught about how to manage God's resources, He told some stories about the rich and others about the poor.

For people in Diane and Neil's position, the Bible has stories like the following.

"Someone in the crowd said to him, 'Teacher, tell my brother to divide the inheritance with me.' Jesus replied, 'Man, who appointed me a judge or an arbiter between you?' Then he said to them, 'Watch out! Be on your guard against all kinds of greed; a man's life does not consist in the abundance of his possessions.' And he told them this parable: 'The ground of a certain rich man produced a good crop. He thought to himself, "What shall I do? I have no place to store my crops."

"'Then he said, "This is what I'll do. I will tear down my barns and build bigger ones, and there I will store all my grain and my goods. And I'll say to myself, 'You have plenty of good things laid up for many years. Take life easy; eat, drink and be merry.'"

"'But God said to him, "You fool! This very night your life will be demanded from you. Then who will get what you have prepared for yourself?"

"'This is how it will be with anyone who stores up things for himself but is not rich toward God'" (Luke 12:13–21).

2. What prompted Jesus to tell this story?

3. What point do you think this story is intended to make?

4. What positive things do you think Jesus would say to Diane and Neil about the way they are managing His money?

5. How do you think Jesus would want Neil and Diane to respond to His story of the rich man?

Diane and Neil are doing a lot of things right, but when people who make as much money as they do still can't afford to be generous, we have to ask why. What is going on inside each of them that decides their priorities? In what areas does the kingdom need to be built within each of them so they can become more able to build the kingdom out in the world?

In Diane's case, although consciously she would wholeheartedly agree that God is willing and able to provide for her, her anxiety suggests that deep down she believes just the opposite. Fear is much more powerful for her than faith. Fear gives her tunnel vision; she's entirely focused on providing comfort and security for herself and her family. She has no attention left over for others, not even for Sharon who works side by side with her.

Neil is driven less by fear than by a desire for status. The house is Diane's status symbol, but it also represents security for her. For Neil, the house, his car, his computer, and the rest of his possessions prove to him and the world that he is succeeding. Neil believes things, not God, give him value.

It will be hard for Diane and Neil to change their financial priorities as long as their deeply felt beliefs are intact—beliefs that they, not God, are providing what they need and that things, not God, determine their value.

6. How do you feel when you think about Neil and
Diane's and Jesus' stories?

_____

_____

_____

Fear and Guilt

Sharon's situation is quite different from Diane's and
Neil's. She's in little danger of collecting too many possessions. She shares Diane's passion for her children's
well-being and her concern for the future, but while
Diane's tendency to worry spurs her to save money,
Sharon's anxiety and guilt are more likely to paralyze
her. Saving money seems impossible. Just making ends
meet is sometimes impossible. Some evenings when several large bills have arrived, especially if one is unexpected (such as for car repairs), Sharon goes into her room,
shuts her door, and sits there, overwhelmed for an hour
or more, unable to move.

Right after telling the story of the rich man and his
bigger barns, Jesus went on to say, "*Therefore I tell you, do
not worry about your life, what you will eat; or about your
body, what you will wear. Life is more than food, and the
body more than clothes. Consider the ravens: They do not
sow or reap, they have no storeroom or barn; yet God feeds
them. And how much more valuable you are than birds!
Who of you by worrying can add a single hour to his life?
Since you cannot do this very little thing, why do you worry
about the rest?*" (Luke 12:22–26).

7. What do you think Jesus would want Sharon to hear from this passage?

_____

_____

_____

_____

Further along in Luke 12, Jesus summed up His teaching on managing God's resources with these words: "*From everyone who has been given much, much will be demanded; and from the one who has been entrusted with much, much more will be asked*" (Luke 12:48).

Sometime later He was teaching in the temple and had occasion to comment further about money management. "*As he looked up, Jesus saw the rich putting their gifts into the temple treasury. He also saw a poor widow put in two very small copper coins. 'I tell you the truth,' he said, 'this poor widow has put in more than all the others. All these people gave their gifts out of their wealth; but she out of her poverty put in all she had to live on'*" (Luke 21:1–4).

8. What do you think Jesus would want Neil, Diane, and Sharon each to learn from this comment about the widow?

_____

_____

_____

_____

_____

_____

_____

9. How does Luke 12:48 apply to Sharon, Diane, and
   Neil?

_____

_____

_____

_____

_____

The Grace Adventure

Guilt comes easily to all of us, but it doesn't always make
us the kinds of people God wants. Even though Diane
feels guilty that she doesn't give enough to the church,
her guilt only motivates her to tune out stewardship ser-
mons. Guilt doesn't make her more generous toward the
church or more openhearted toward Sharon. Only a
deep awareness of God's grace—His patience with her
anxiety and self-centeredness and His power to over-
come her habits—will move Diane to start asking the
right questions about her priorities.

In the same way, guilt only paralyzes Sharon. If she could begin to grasp that God desires to lavish His grace on her, she might gain the emotional energy to look for creative solutions to her budget problems. She might not be ashamed to ask Diane for help because she would see that Diane needs her too. She might respect herself more if she could believe that God would be excited if she started saving even $25 a month or gave even $15 a month to His work.

10. In what ways do you identify with Diane, Neil, or Sharon?

_____

_____

11. How do you think Luke 12:48 applies to you?

_____

_____

12. Share with the group what situation you need God's grace for today. Then take a few minutes of silence to pray. (If you have time, you can divide into groups of three and pray for your partners.)

During the Week

- What help do you need in managing your resources that doesn't include borrowing money?

Whom can you ask for help? Consider someone in your group.

• Contemplate Jesus' statement: *"From the one who has been entrusted with much, much more will be asked"* (Luke 12:48). Ask yourself how it makes you feel: guilty? grateful for grace? Ask yourself what you should do about it.

• Read session 5 before your next meeting.

RULING THE EARTH

1. When you hear about an environmental dispute, what emotions do you typically feel? Anger? Boredom? Helplessness? Excitement?

_____

_____

Subduing and Ruling

Many members of the Deep Ecology movement blame Christian doctrine for the abuse of land, water, and air in the past two thousand years. They claim Christians use passages like Genesis 1:28 to justify exploiting earth's resources for the short-term gain of humans, regardless of the long-term cost to plants and animals. In session 1 we read, "*God blessed them and said to them, 'Be fruitful and increase in number; fill the earth and subdue it. Rule over the fish of the sea and the birds of the air and over every living creature that moves on the ground*'" (Genesis 1:28).

Deep Ecologists reject the notion that humans have the right to "subdue" the earth and "rule over" animals. To them, those terms suggest the careless self-centeredness of conquerors subduing and abusing helpless victims. Deep Ecologists go so far as to deny that humans outrank animals in any moral way. They believe a human life is no more valuable than an animal life in any situation. Consequently, they decry testing drugs on animals and using animal insulin for diabetics. They believe earth's human population should be reduced drastically so that we will not encroach on animal and plant habitats any more than we already have.

Deep Ecologists represent the far end of the environ-mentalist spectrum. However, many more moderate environmentalists cringe at terms like "subdue" and "rule over." This is not just an academic question. If God owns the Earth and has assigned us to manage His prop-erty, we have to ask ourselves precisely what He means in Genesis 1:28. The answer will affect how we approach all kinds of questions that affect our lives daily.

For example, logging companies in the Northwest want to manage forests so that loggers will have jobs and companies can supply lumber to their customers. Their opponents charge that loggers' priorities threaten the habitats of certain animals. If God has given all of us together the responsibility to manage the northwestern forests according to His priorities, we have to ask our-selves what those priorities are and how to balance them.

In Idaho, ranchers clash with environmentalists over how to use federally owned rangeland. Large agricultural companies battle with environmentalists over how to treat South American rain forests. Manufacturers in some states feel unable to produce their products cost effectively because of laws regarding air and water pollu-tion. Are the laws too strict or too loose? And what about recycling? Is it worth the effort and money it costs? All of these issues challenge us to examine our jobs as God's land managers.

2. Name an environmental issue that affects you directly. Without going into your views, tell the group briefly what you *feel* when you think about that issue.

_____

_____

_____

3. What do you think God meant when He instructed us to "subdue" the earth and "rule over" animals?

_____

_____

_____

_____

Most of the Bible concerns God's dealings with people. However, a few passages express how God feels about animals. The book of Job is a dramatic poem—a poem with various characters, like in a play. In the following Scripture passage, God responds to Job's charge that God doesn't know how to run the world properly. Notice the way God's questions pile up, one on top of another on top of another.

"*Do you know when the mountain goats give birth? Do you watch when the doe bears her fawn? Do you count the months till they bear? Do you know the time they give birth?*

They crouch down and bring forth their young; their labor pains are ended. Their young thrive and grow strong in the wilds; they leave and do not return.

"Who let the wild donkey go free? Who untied his ropes? I gave him the wasteland as his home, the salt flats as his habitat. He laughs at the commotion in the town; he does not hear a driver's shout. He ranges the hills for his pasture and searches for any green thing.

"Will the wild ox consent to serve you? Will he stay by your manger at night? Can you hold him to the furrow with a harness? Will he till the valleys behind you? Will you rely on him for his great strength? Will you leave your heavy work to him? Can you trust him to bring in your grain and gather it to your threshing floor?" (Job 39:1–12).

4. How does this barrage of questions affect you?
   What impact do you think God is after?

_____

_____

_____

_____

The Scripture story continues.

"The wings of the ostrich flap joyfully, but they cannot compare with the pinions and feathers of the stork. She lays her eggs on the ground and lets them warm in the sand, unmindful that a foot may crush them, that some wild animal may trample them. She treats her young harshly, as if they were not hers; she cares not that her labor was in vain, for

God did not endow her with wisdom or give her a share of good sense. Yet when she spreads her feathers to run, she laughs at horse and rider.

"Do you give the horse his strength or clothe his neck with a flowing mane? Do you make him leap like a locust, striking terror with his proud snorting? He paws fiercely, rejoicing in his strength, and charges into the fray. He laughs at fear, afraid of nothing; he does not shy away from the sword. The quiver rattles against his side, along with the flashing spear and lance. In frenzied excitement he eats up the ground; he cannot stand still when the trumpet sounds. At the blast of the trumpet he snorts, 'Aha!' He catches the scent of battle from afar, the shout of commanders and the battle cry.

"Does the hawk take flight by your wisdom and spread his wings toward the south? Does the eagle soar at your command and build his nest on high? He dwells on a cliff and stays there at night; a rocky crag is his stronghold. From there he seeks out his food; his eyes detect it from afar. His young ones feast on blood, and where the slain are, there is he" (Job 39:13–30).

5. After reading Job 39, how much would you say God values animals? What gives you that impression?

_____

_____

_____

_____

_____

Psalm 104 describes how God cares for the natural world.

"He makes springs pour water into the ravines; it flows between the mountains. They give water to all the beasts of the field; the wild donkeys quench their thirst. The birds of the air nest by the waters; they sing among the branches. He waters the mountains from his upper chambers; the earth is satisfied by the fruit of his work.

"He makes grass grow for the cattle, and plants for man to cultivate—bringing forth food from the earth: wine that gladdens the heart of man, oil to make his face shine, and bread that sustains his heart. The trees of the Lord are well watered, the cedars of Lebanon that he planted. There the birds make their nests; the stork has its home in the pine trees. The high mountains belong to the wild goats; the crags are a refuge for the coneys.

"The moon marks off the seasons, and the sun knows when to go down. You bring darkness, it becomes night, and all the beasts of the forest prowl. The lions roar for their prey and seek their food from God. The sun rises, and they steal away; they return and lie down in their dens. Then man goes out to his work, to his labor until evening.

"How many are your works, O Lord! In wisdom you made them all; the earth is full of your creatures. There is the sea, vast and spacious, teeming with creatures beyond number—living things both large and small. There the ships go to and fro, and the leviathan, which you formed to frolic there.

"These all look to you to give them their food at the proper time. When you give it to them, they gather it up; when you open your hand, they are satisfied with good things.

"When you hide your face, they are terrified; when you take away their breath, they die and return to the dust. When *you send your Spirit, they are created, and you renew the face of the earth"* (Psalm 104:10–30).

6. How does Psalm 104 describe relationships among God, the natural world, and humans?

_____

_____

_____

_____

_____

Jesus told His hearers, *"How much more valuable you are than birds!"* (Luke 12:24). *"God said, 'Let us make man in our image, in our likeness, and let them rule over the fish of the sea and birds of the air, over the livestock, over all the earth, and over all the creatures that move along the ground'"* (Genesis 1:26).

7. Which of the following statements do you think reflect biblical attitudes, and which do not? Explain your reasoning.

❑ Our needs always outweigh animal needs.

❑ Animal needs always outweigh our needs.

❑ God highly values animals but even more highly values us.

❑ Because God values us more than animals, we can use animals however we want.

❑ God holds us responsible to rule over the earth
   with great care for its nonhuman inhabitants.

❑ Ruling the earth well will require us to make
   some sacrifices.

8. How do you feel about bearing part of the
   responsibility for ruling the earth?

_____

_____

_____

9. What is one way in which you as an individual or
   group can exercise that responsibility?

_____

_____

_____

The Grace Adventure

Most of us feel challenged enough managing a household,
never mind a planet. Forests, rangeland, water, air—it's
all so complex. God knows our limitations and forgives
our failures, but He also believes in our abilities as men
and women who bear His image, especially when we
work together to accomplish what we cannot do alone.

10. Take some time in prayer to tell God how you feel

about bearing part of the responsibility for a planet. Ask Him for wisdom to know what you can and should do. If specific issues are on your minds, pray about them.

During the Week

- As you watch the news this week or go about your daily business, watch for an issue that involves managing the earth's resources. Take some time to pray about this issue. Ask God to give wisdom to the people involved. Ask what your part might be.

- Think about how Genesis 1:28 applies to the decisions you face this week.

- Read session 6 before your next meeting.

SHREWDNESS

1. What environmental issues have you encountered since discussing session 5?

_____

_____

Using Our Heads

When Jesus sent His twelve disciples out on their first kingdom-building expedition, He instructed them, "*I am sending you out like sheep among wolves. Therefore be as shrewd as snakes and as innocent as doves*" (Matthew 10:16). The dove symbolized the Holy Spirit (Matthew 3:16); the snake represented the devil in Eden (Genesis 3:1). Jesus wanted His followers to be as ethical as God but as smart as Satan.

Shrewdness is not normally considered a Christian virtue, perhaps because too seldom we see it coupled with ethics. The following is one of Jesus' most provocative stories about stewardship.

"*There was a rich man whose manager was accused of wasting his possessions. So he called him in and asked him, 'What is this I hear about you? Give an account of your management, because you cannot be manager any longer.'*

"*The manager said to himself, 'What shall I do now? My master is taking away my job. I'm not strong enough to dig, and I'm ashamed to beg—I know what I'll do so that, when I*

CARETAKERS OF GOD'S BLESSINGS

lose my job here, people will welcome me into their houses.'

"So he called in each one of his master's debtors. He asked the first, 'How much do you owe my master?'

"'Eight hundred gallons of olive oil,' he replied.

"The manager told him, 'Take your bill, sit down quickly, and make it four hundred.'

"Then he asked the second, 'And how much do you owe?'

"'A thousand bushels of wheat,' he replied.

"He told him, 'Take your bill and make it eight hundred.'

"The master commended the dishonest manager because he had acted shrewdly. For the people of this world are more shrewd in dealing with their own kind than are the people of the light. I tell you, use worldly wealth to gain friends for yourselves, so that when it is gone, you will be welcomed into eternal dwellings" (Luke 16:1–9).

2. What questions does this story raise in your mind?

_____

_____

_____

Generations of Bible readers have been stunned to find Jesus (through the master) *praising* the manager's shrewdness, rather than condemning his dishonesty. The story was intended to shock its hearers, and it usually does. But Jesus' point is that this manager knew how to read the handwriting on the wall. He knew his days were numbered, and he was smart enough to use worldly wealth (NASB: *"the mammon of unrighteousness"*) to win friends where it counted.

Where, Jesus wants to know, are those of God's people who are smart enough to see that their own day of reckoning is coming and yet are shrewdly using unrighteous money to win friends in the kingdom of righteousness? Given the urgency of the kingdom—the fact that we are all running out of time—why aren't God's people more creative and insightful in their use of wealth?

A shrewd manager can do a lot more with few resources than a pretentious manager can with many resources. For example, in 1983 Ganga Stone brought a bag of groceries to a man dying of AIDS. Arriving at his house, she realized he was far too sick to cook for himself, so she started phoning his friends. Soon this man was receiving a hot meal every day. But Ganga met others like him. With less than $10 as start-up money, she created God's Love We Deliver, which in 1994 organized 1,700 volunteers to feed more than 600 shut-ins a day. Forty of New York's best restaurants donated food, thanks to Ganga's talent for persuasion.

"Well done, good and faithful servant! You have been faithful with a few things; I will put you in charge of many things" (Matthew 25:21). Ganga was faithful with $10 and a gift for persuasion; God eventually entrusted her with a $5.5 million organization.

Not all of us will find ourselves managing that much of God's wealth in this lifetime, but any of us can cultivate Ganga's creativity. Along with a willingness to risk and a commitment to God's priorities, shrewdness or creativity is an essential mind-set for a member of God's management team.

What would this kind of shrewdness look like in Diane's life? If she worried less about her own family's security, she could take Sharon to lunch and ask her about her life and her needs. Together they might think of some creative ways to solve Sharon's budget problems.

Neil and Diane might be able to connect Sharon with people in their church who have the skills Sharon lacks. They might find Sharon needs some moral support in planning and sticking to a budget. Maybe Sharon's budget would work if she didn't have to pay for routine car maintenance such as oil changes, and a friend of Neil's would be willing to do that for her. Perhaps Neil and Diane could go with Sharon to select new tires. The possibilities are endless when God's people put their heads together and think beyond familiar boundaries.

Fear and embarrassment paralyze creative thinking. Courage and trust in God's grace free us to be shrewd. Sometimes it's hard to muster courage when we feel alone; that's why we're exhorted to *"encourage one another"* (1 Thessalonians 5:11)—literally to give each other courage.

We're a management *team*, and we need each other. So even if Sharon doesn't know any Dianes, if she knows one other single mother who also struggles, she can team up with her. Together they might visit one of their pastors to find someone who will think creatively with them.

If we are made in God's image, then each of us carries a spark of the genius that enabled God to think up a universe. If we bear His image, then any of us can cultivate a tiny seed of the shrewdness by which God used the cross of Christ to outsmart the devil. God believes in our management potential, or He wouldn't have given us the job. We need to believe in it too.

3. Jesus said, *"Use worldly wealth to gain friends for yourselves."* How could Neil and Diane use their resources to win friends in really high places?

_____

_____

_____

_____

_____

4. Does this sound like buying your way into heaven? Why do you say that?

_____

_____

_____

_____

5. Why is it often hard for us to remember, when it comes time to make a financial decision, that we need friends in heaven more urgently than we need friends on earth?

_____

_____

_____

_____

6. Innovative businesses use techniques such as *brainstorming* and *storyboarding* to help people generate unexpected ideas. (Ever wondered how somebody thought up Velcro?) You can buy books on how to foster creative thinking, but for now try the following exercise. You'll need index cards, markers, a bulletin board, and pushpins—or index cards, markers, and tape.

   a. Think of something you believe God wants done. It might be "Dan and Barbara save money on car repairs" or "Fix the church roof" or "Provide a healthy environment for kids after school." Have someone in the group write this goal on a card. Choose someone else to be responsible for posting cards. That person should post the card at the top of the bulletin board or tape it to a wall where you have plenty of space for more cards.

   b. The person responsible for posting cards is also the timekeeper. For fifteen minutes, everyone else has to think up as many ideas as possible that would contribute to the goal and write each idea on a separate card. When you've written an idea, give the card to the cardposter/timekeeper and say your idea aloud. The cardposter posts the idea. Zany ideas are okay: "An anonymous donor gives the church $5,000." Criticizing or making fun of anyone's ideas is completely off-limits. There are no "bad" ideas. For fifteen minutes, anything goes.

c. At the end of fifteen minutes, review the results.
    You probably have a lot of useless rocks, but you
    might find one or two gemstones among them.
    When you really shut down your internal critics
    and give your minds free rein, you may be
    amazed at what develops.

7. Take a few minutes to assess what you've learned
    from this study. What new ideas or perspectives
    have you gained?

_____

_____

_____

_____

8. How has this study affected the way you've been
    viewing and treating your resources during the
    past few weeks?

_____

_____

_____

_____

_____

9. Where would you like to go from here with what you've learned?

_____

_____

_____

_____

_____

_____

The Grace Adventure

Stewardship is a big, responsible job, whether you're managing a rain forest or a household budget. We don't need to let the size of the job overwhelm us, though. The Holy Spirit lives inside us to train and counsel us, and the Bible offers us a wealth of wisdom. We also can draw upon each other for feedback and encouragement. We won't be instant experts, but together we can learn to become effective managers of God's resources.

10. Give everyone in the group an opportunity to thank God for what they have learned or to ask for wisdom about a particular issue. Close by asking the Holy Spirit to fill all of you with courage, shrewdness, and a commitment to God's priorities in managing His world.

During the Week

- Review the verses you have been focusing on during this study. What do you see in them now that you didn't see when you started?

* * * *

"So then, men ought to regard us as servants of Christ and as those entrusted with the secret things of God. Now it is required that those who have been given a trust must prove faithful" (1 Corinthians 4:1–2).

Christian
Financial
Concepts

Teaching | Biblical Principles of Managing Money

Larry Burkett, founder and president of Christian Financial Concepts, is the best-selling author of 37 books on business and personal finances and 2 novels. He also hosts two radio programs broadcast on hundreds of stations worldwide.

Larry holds degrees in marketing and finance, and for several years served as a manager in the space program at Cape Canaveral, Florida. He also has been vice president of an electronics manufacturing firm. Larry's education, business experience, and solid understanding of God's Word enable him to give practical, Bible-based financial counsel to families, churches, and businesses.

Founded in 1976, Christian Financial Concepts is a nonprofit, nondenominational ministry dedicated to helping God's people gain a clear understanding of how to manage their money according to scriptural principles. While practical assistance is provided on many levels, the purpose of CFC is simply *to bring glory to God by freeing His people from financial bondage so they may serve Him to their utmost.*

One major avenue of ministry involves the training of volunteers in budget and debt counseling and linking them with financially troubled families and individuals through a nationwide referral network. CFC also provides financial management seminars and workshops for churches and other groups. (Formats available include audio, video, video with moderator, and live instruction.) A full line of printed and audio-visual materials related to money management is available through CFC's materials department (1-800-722-1976).

Career Pathways, another outreach of Christian Financial Concepts, helps teenagers and adults find their occupational calling. The Career Pathways "Testing Package" gauges a person's work priorities, skills, vocational interests, and personality. Reports in each of these areas define a person's strengths, weaknesses, and unique, God-given pattern for work.

For further information about the ministry of Christian Financial Concepts, write to:

Christian Financial Concepts
PO Box 2377
Gainesville, GA 30503-2377

The Financial Planning Workbook

This workbook includes practical advice about managing your finances and provides a series of easy-to-follow worksheets that allow you to structure and maintain your family's budget. Larry shows you where to start, how to stay on track, and even addresses special budgeting problems. Extra worksheets are included.

The Word on Finances

This useful tool contains a collection of relevant Scriptures arranged under eight comprehensive headings. Larry's practical wisdom opens each of the more than seventy topical selections.

Debt-Free Living

This book is for anyone whose money ran out before the month did. Again. Or even if your financial situation hasn't reached a crisis point, you will benefit from Larry's wise counsel. Through case studies of several marriages helped through proper financial counsel, Larry shows how to become and remain debt-free. He warns about the kinds of credit to avoid and provides specific how-to's for solving debt problems. *Debt-Free Living* remains a best-seller, with more than 150,000 copies in print.

How to Manage Your Money

There is so much religious "folklore" regarding money that few Christians understand God's true will in finances. But the Scriptures have plenty to say about how we should handle the funds entrusted to us. There are more than 700 direct references to money in the Bible and hundreds more indirect references. *How to Manage Your Money*, a Bible study by Larry Burkett, brings many of these references to light as it introduces Christians to the "scriptural" view of finances. This workbook covers such topics as stewardship, short- and long-range planning, tithing, and much more.

Your Finances in Changing Times

With more than a million copies in print, this book is a perfect introduction to basic financial management. It is a complete money guide, offering biblical concepts and practical suggestions for building a sound financial program. Learn to plan for the future, get out or stay out of debt, and much more.